MW00957811

A Pilot's Guide
For
Fearful Flyers

Captain Chris Manno

Dark Horse
Books

Fort Worth, Texas USA

A PILOT'S GUIDE FOR FEARFUL FLYERS

Dark Horse Books

ISBN-13: 978-1975882402
ISBN-10: 1975882407

Blog; JetHead.Wordpress.com

Twitter: @chris_manno

FOREWORD

For every fearful flyer, there's often one or more family or friends who are therefore also grounded. Meanwhile, surface transportation eats up vacation days and limits travel options. Many destinations, including a vacation abroad, are out of the question for everyone, not just the fearful flyer.

This book is about empowerment, letting the fearful flyer displace dread with facts and insider knowledge to make choices based on what they want, rather than some unknown they can't envision or don't understand.

I've been a pilot at the world's largest airline for more than 32 years, over 26 of them as captain, and I empathize with fearful flyers. I've seen firsthand that even the most nervous flyers can be reassured to the extent that at least allows them to fly in reasonable comfort and ease, thereby opening up a whole new and broad world of travel possibilities.

So here are my best techniques to engage the entire process, to understand all aspects of your flight and most importantly, to give flyers an inside view of what's going on in the cockpit and what they need to do on board and especially, leading up to a flight, so they can better understand their flight, what's happening and when, and why.

As the title states, this book is by "A Pilot," me, and I claim no broad authority other than my decades as an airline captain and thousands of hours aloft dealing with all the elements of air travel, including fearful flyers. I'm not the "ace of the base" hotshot pilot, and I don't care to be. I've always worked hard to be a thorough, careful, skilled and competent journeyman aviator. That perspective can help you, too.

Welcome aboard, and let's get started. -CM

A PILOT'S GUIDE FOR FEARFUL FLYERS

CONTENTS

A PILOT'S GUIDE FOR FEARFUL FLYERS

ACKNOWLEDGMENTS

I am forever indebted to the Virginia Military Institute, my alma mater, and my Aerospace Sciences professor Colonel John D. Sullivan, USAF, for getting me into USAF Pilot Training even without 20-20 vision; to Captain Clark T. "Curly" Culp for teaching me to fly a T-38, to Chip, Coke, Animal and the entire Wolf Pack Flight for the best aviating and drinking ever in Texas and beyond; to the American Airlines captains who endured having with me as their First Officer while showing me by example how to be a captain; to the hundreds of excellent American Airlines First Officers who continue to make me look a lot smarter than I really am as captain; to the world's best flight attendants who've put up with me for decades, to the dozens of AA Flight Academy instructor pilots and Check Airmen who've sharpened my flight skills year after year; to those pilots who tolerated me as a Check Airman when I learned from them more than I ever taught, and finally, to the Laws of Gravity that have given me a pass for most of my life.

Truly, the sky is *not* the limit—it's just a great place to be.

--CM

A PILOT'S GUIDE FOR FEARFUL FLYERS

1. THE BIG PICTURE

Fearful? Don't feel like The Lone Ranger: everyone at some point has a degree of anxiety about flight, which is natural. Even among aviation professionals at all levels, a healthy respect for the reality of flight is the bedrock of safety and common sense. Anxiety is simply a natural offshoot of that very human urge for self-preservation.

When as an Air Force pilot I studied Flight Safety and Accident Investigation at the USC School of Flight Safety, they constantly referred to the "2 mile per hour man," because that's our DNA. Flying at 500 miles an hour is unnatural, and our physiology and psychology is engineered to avoid movement beyond our design envelope.

Anxiety naturally goes with the unknown territory, which flight is at some point for all flyers. When I reached the syllabus phase in USAF Flight School that called for the instructor pilot to induce a flat spin from over twenty-five thousand feet basically straight down to ten thousand feet, I was "concerned" to say the least, because that maneuver for me was an unknown: I'd never twirled like a record on a turntable vertically four miles straight down.

Add to that the syllabus requirement that I should, upon reaching ten thousand feet, be capable (according to the lesson objectives) of applying the complex, multi-step recovery procedure to break out of the flat spin I'd memorized. The feeling that comes to mind is what I was told by a space shuttle astronaut about launch: "Everyone aboard was either scared shitless or lying."

So when the big moment arrived, when the instructor pilot asked, "Are you ready," I nodded, keeping faith in my belief that if everyone else could perform this maneuver, so could I. Add to that my 22-year-old self's latent *hubris* (I honestly believed I'd rather die than fail to win Air Force pilot wings) and I pushed myself beyond the boundary of fear—which isn't to say I didn't have it. I sure did.

Once the spin commenced, the effect was, honestly, much ado about nothing: the sensation was as if the world was spinning around us and we were perfectly still. I could see the altimeter unwind as we plummeted, I noted the compass card rotating like a merry-go-round. But I was fine, the jet was fine, and I knew right then and there that the apprehension about this extreme flight maneuver is actually worse than the maneuver itself in real life.

Of course, I'm sure I screwed up the recovery, at least my first time—I said I wasn't the ace of the base—but the more important lesson was about the psychological effects of anticipation versus reality. A few folks were unable to see that crucial perspective and either resigned or were washed out.

Psychology is only half of the self-preservation urge that has to be dealt with to function effectively when challenging the unknown. We all discovered that physiology was an even more formidable barrier: the body's sense of balance does not do well adapting to aerobatics. A handful of my classmates were gifted by nature with an individual equilibrium that seemed impervious to loops, rolls and high G-force maneuvers. I was not among them.

Mustaches disappeared around the Flight Room because food began to appear post-flight in tiny pieces embedded during the awkward demands of flying a jet while vomiting. Breakfast choices were modified to consider not only how the food would taste going down, but also coming back up (orange juice burned, as I recall) in flight. It was miserable. Making you fly even while barfing was part of the syllabus: if you can't hack it, you'll never solo—so fly, or quit; your choice. Several more quit.

But believing I'd rather be dead than wash out, I wasn't going to let nausea stand in the way of my silver wings. The Flight Surgeon prescribed for those of us suffering air sickness a combination of Dramamine for the nausea and Dexadrine to counteract the drowsiness side effect of the Dramamine.

That helped a lot. But the big revelation, as with the psychological barriers, was simple: adaptation. After a while, my system adapted to high-G loads and aerobatic maneuvers. I no longer needed the Dramamine, although those of us who had the Dexadrine kept taking the prescription and were wide-awake for predawn flights, while the other guys were drag-assed tired. But the playing field eventually levelled once again when our prescriptions ran out and the "Witch Doctor," as we called the Flight Surgeon, refused to issue refills (I did ask).

But the point is, everyone must brave some level of anxiety, some fear, some psychological and even physiological barriers if they're to adapt and succeed at any unknown precipice. You've done that already in your life thus far and I promise you, this fear of flying challenge will yield in the same way to determination, knowledge (then it's not the unknown), fortitude, encouragement from others and finally—adaptation. You will succeed. You will move onward, and upward, literally. You may have toast crumbs in your mustache at first (shave it off, regrow it later), and you may not accomplish the perfect recovery on the first spin. But eventually, you will.

In subsequent chapters I'll highlight for you an

insider view of what goes on before, during and after a flight so that we can reduce the "unknown" part of your fear. We'll also look at strategies to prepare for both the psychological and physiological challenges that flying can present to you. It's a proven fact that the more you know, the less the "unknown" will affect you.

Read on, reflect, and let's learn together how to chip away at your very natural, normal fear of flying.

Quick Reference Summary

- Fear of flying is natural, normal, and manageable.
- As humans, we're designed with both psychological and physiological defenses geared towards self-preservation, which is good.
- Aviators at all levels experience anxiety about flying, but learn to manage both risks and stress.
- Adaptation is key to feeling at home in the sky, and that just takes perseverance and when available, the proper pharmaceuticals.
- Orange juice burns when coming back up.

Optional Sardonic Cartoon

2. IT"S ALL ABOUT YOU

No, seriously—it really *is*: no other area of either transportation or technology has ever been more specifically and consistently engineered, designed, regulated and enforced with *you*, the passenger, as the focal point than modern air travel.

Sure, there's a National Highway Safety Commission and various government agencies regulating driver's licenses, and there are standards for auto and truck manufacturers. But those are nothing compared to the rigid airworthiness standards to which all commercial aircraft are built and tested, and nowhere near the year-round scrutiny given to pilots through unrelenting FAA checks in flight, in the doctor's office, and in recurring background checks.

That's a wonderful, unique thing in an increasingly complex and high speed world of transportation, and safety statistics show how air travel has advanced above and beyond all other modes of travel.

There's a learning curve in the airline industry that has improved steadily since the early days of airline flight in the 1930s: accident rates have steadily dropped year over year and aircraft and engine reliability has increased in a parallel vector.

I recently had an aviation magazine editor ask me what I would cite as the primary cause of engine malfunctions that lead to a flight cancellation. I answered honestly that I've been flying on my particular fleet for over six years and I've *never* experienced an engine malfunction in that entire time.

That wasn't so about twenty years ago, before aircraft and engine technology had advanced to its present state of reliability. But that's the aviation learning curve: since the late 1990s, the advent of constant, data-linked engine monitoring now sends a wide array of engine parameters from the jet in cruise to a maintenance and engineering data analysis center that catches nascent faults and liabilities way before they become failures.

Last month I received a message in flight from our maintenance and engineering center asking me to check the vibration reading on a particular engine, because it was reading a bit high to them on the ground. Engine failures "on the wing" as we call them, are so rare that they actually make the news when they happen.

There's a learning curve success story: decade after decade, we've developed new technology and hand-in-hand with strict regulatory enforcement, the airline biz has lowered the flight risks and added new layers of accident prevention and aircraft reliability.

By contrast, the automobile and highway transportation sector's safety record has stagnated and even regressed over the same time period as air travel has improved: the traffic accident and fatality statistics have actually worsened as more cars hit the road and as speed limits are raised. Little is done to regulate or retest drivers other than observation and apprehension by a law enforcement officer. Even less is done to determine accident cause factors and develop technological and regulatory improvements to lower passenger risks.

By comparison, the air travel safety imperative is unprecedented, the standard uncompromisingly high: everything involved in air travel is geared toward passenger safety. Licensing of pilots, certification of training, manufacturing standards and operating restrictions for airlines are so constrained that if an equal measure were applied to the highways and drivers, the roads would be vastly safer—and nearly empty.

No government inspector climbs into a big tractor trailer rig to ride along and evaluate a trucker firsthand several times every year.

There's not a government regulator assigned to a trucking company to monitor records, safety and training not to mention vehicle maintenance and repairs. Truck manufacturers have some rudimentary safety and fuel mileage standards, but the vehicles are not inspected by government licensed and tested mechanics daily.

No automobile driver is required to renew a driver's license every nine months with a graded road test, plus oral and written exams, not to mention a government controlled physical exam with a specified doctor reporting results immediately to the government, never mind the periodic background check and the no-notice, no-refusal "we're going to ride with you" spot evaluation.

By contrast, your flight crew—front (pilots) and back (flight attendants) are constantly monitored, tested and certified.

That why air travel safety has improved annually while highway safety muddles along or actually regresses, and annual traffic fatalities remain at staggeringly high rates. Yet, the paradox remains: hardly a mention of "fear of driving" is made even in the face of thousands of lives lost on the highway annually, while fear of flying is a very real dilemma.

All of aviation is not safety-driven as is airline flying. In the military, the mission was primary, my safety as a pilot secondary to that. We accepted that, and many still do flying for our military.

By contrast, the entire airline aircraft design, engineering (we'll talk about that later) and manufacturing industry all telescopes down to one objective: *you*, and your safety. Same goes for the training, licensing, nonstop testing and evaluation of pilots, dispatchers, air traffic controllers and aircraft mechanics. In military terms, you and your flight *are* the mission.

That's the compelling force that drives the airline industry, and it's all about you. While that might be hard to see when you're enduring the hassles of security, and check-in, and boarding, it's a powerful awareness to keep in your hip pocket: rest assured, everything about the jet you fly on, the crew that flies and maintains it, and the air traffic controllers who guide it have *you* as their focus. You are the mission.

So, recognize this windfall for what it is. Compare your clear priority in airline travel with the abject failure that is highway safety, a risk you live with every day. Air travel is actually your safest place, the one technological juggernaut where it really is all about you.

We'll go into more specifics on who's flying your jet, but for now, keep in your hip pocket the monumental safety success that has been designed around you the passenger, making air travel the safest mode of transportation you will ever take.

Remember the objective stated in the foreword to this book: empowerment is the key here. You've made a choice to learn about flight, to consider whether you want to give it a try. That's real control because at any point, you can stop. You really are in charge and anything but powerless.

Stay with that decision for now, knowing it's not set in stone—you can change your mind—and let's expand your fact-based knowledge of airline flying.

Quick Reference Summary

- Aircraft design, engineering and manufacturing is regulated with you as the central priority.
- The air travel learning curve in the United States has refined the industry and minimized risk factors over many decades.

- High-tech, data-linked systems monitor aircraft systems performance and preempt failures.
- By comparison, the risk factors associated with everyday highway traffic far outweigh the well-managed factors of air travel.

3. WHO"S FLYING YOUR JET?

I'm a fairly typical example of who you'll find in your airliner's cockpit. I'm a college graduate, served as an Air Force officer and pilot for seven years then came to work for my airline. At my airline, ex-military pilots comprise over half of our seniority list.

Other possible career entry tracks include a civilian path that typically involves years as a flight instructor, then a step up to a commuter carrier or a cargo operator, building enough flight time and experience to be hired by a major airline.

Those are the two major paths and everyone seems to fall somewhere along that continuum. My son was an Air Force officer but didn't fly in the military. He worked to attain all of his flight ratings on his own, then flight-instructed for over a thousand hours, then was hired by a regional airline. Today, he's a first officer flying Airbus-320 jets for a major carrier. Different entry paths, but we both ended up in exactly the same place.

Once hired by an airline, there's really no qualitative difference between pilots based on their previous career path. All pilot candidates get scrutinized during the interview process and once hired, we're all the same.

As a new hire pilot, I spent a brief period as flight engineer, a position that no longer exists in today's more automated cockpits, then I became a First Officer ("FO," as we say), first on smaller, narrow-body (means: single aisle) aircraft. I moved up to widebody FO, then to captain where I've been for the past 26 years and counting.

Regardless of how a pilot gets to a major carrier, the track afterward can be summed up in one word: standardization. For example, I flew up to Newark last week on my regular trip, which was DFW to Newark, then back to DFW. After we landed in Newark, my FO packed his flight gear and deplaned because he was at the maximum flight duty limit (I'll explain that later).

Another First Officer from the New York pilot crew base stepped aboard and off we went back to DFW. What's remarkable about that is this: we have over 15,000 pilots at my airline, and we are so standardized in procedures, policies, and standard practices that there was a perfect gear mesh from the moment he stepped into the cockpit. That's standardization.

I like to joke with flight attendants that I'm "the interchangeable pilot man:" we look alike, we think alike, we act alike. We strive to do things the exact same, standard and correct way each flight, each procedure, each minute.

Our world is recursive: we drill over and over, refine our skills, review, retrain, reinforce. Our thinking is centripetal: we wrap layers of conformance with compliance and ever-increasing standardization. That's the opposite of the creative, artsy world that thinks and acts centrifugally, pushing outward, exploring. We work inward, strengthening and reinforcing the flight procedures we know.

Pilot-world is weird that way. We're grounded in precise procedures and compliance with standard practices. The profession is crafted that way to ensure that our operation complies with the best, safest practices in the airline industry.

There's not an iota of "that's not how we do it in the New York base" or any other falsely justified variance, which helps me do my job: I know exactly what the other pilot thinks and will do in every given situation. That's an asset to us all and we guard that jealously.

In fact, our pilot union—as with most airline pilot unions—has a national Professional Standards committee with trusted pilot members at every crew base. If anyone even begins to stray from the best professional standards, they'll get a call, they'll have a conversation that steers them back to the centerline of professional standards we all rely upon.

Add to that the base Chief Pilots who play a supervisory role, always on duty and ready to support a crew with guidance and directives, but as importantly to provide some quality control to the human aspect of the cockpit crew. Again, a series of checks and balances, seeing beyond the boilerplate requirements and looking even deeper to seek out problems in our flight operations that could be improved with additional guidance and training.

The Chiefs have leeway to help pilots in order to intercept distractions that could affect crew function. If a pilot has problems at home, Chiefs will send them home to work on the problems rather than bringing them into the cockpit, degrading crew performance.

Human factors awareness goes even deeper, because we all realize that perfect compliance is jeopardized by physical or emotional stress. Every pilot at my airline knows this and has every reason *not* to fly when not a hundred percent both physically and emotionally. Before each flight leg, every pilot certifies via cockpit computer, iPad or smart phone that we are physically and emotionally fit to fly—not every work day, *every single flight*. If not, we are removed and replaced at no penalty to the pilot so as to encourage self-reporting of fitness accurately.

Every pilot trains and retrains. The recurring training cycle at my airline is every nine months and we like to joke wryly that this is the only career field where you have to reapply for your job every year. We have days of classroom refresher training, then the flight simulator practice and finally, the evaluation.

The simulator training is done in full-motion, advanced sims. There's a practice simulator session that lasts about 6 hours total that allows us to realistically experience malfunctions and apply corrective procedures to land safely. That's followed by another session the next day that includes an evaluator. The Federal Aviation Administration has a standard list of objectives and standards that must be satisfactorily demonstrated or the pilot's certificate is suspended.

If that happens, which it does very rarely, the pilot is given remedial training, then a reevaluation. If that's not satisfactory, the FAA will decide whether or not to permanently revoke a pilot's flight privileges. Brutal, but that's as it should be: we're a team on the flight deck and no one who can't meet the flight standard belongs there. When I was in Air Force Flight Training we used to joke that we were always just two rides from the door, meaning, flunk or as we say, "bust" two flight evaluations in a row and you are washed out. It's about the same here, year after year.

Once we successfully pass the flight eval, the second half of the Day 2 simulator is spent on advanced training: challenging crosswinds, high-altitude airports, short runways, mountainous approaches, windshear, upset maneuvers (if some anomaly were to flip our jet, here's how we'll flip it back), stalls, single engine approaches—all things you couldn't practice safely in a real jet, but which you can experience and practice very realistically in a simulator.

I always come out of my recurrent training, which we like to refer to as our "annual beating," smarter, humbler, and better prepared to fly your jet safely.

Once the Annual Beating is done, I expect multiple real-time FAA evaluators on the cockpit jumpseat evaluating me in flight, plus no-notice company Check Airmen riding the jumpseat and grading my whole management of the flight from brake release to chocks are put in front of the wheels at our destination. Finally, my airline fields an array of trained safety observers who blanket our flights with evaluators simply taking notes: what works well in the cockpit? What might work better?

As I mentioned elsewhere, every pilot gets an annual physical exam from an FAA Flight Surgeon (captains must have a physical every six months) and all pilots over 40 must have an FAA medical-provided EKG that is transmitted directly to the FAA medical department for analysis as it is recorded.

Part of the medical exam is a detailed and ongoing history that includes all prescriptions and medical procedures, doctor visits and condition changes from the last physical. Pilots must also report any traffic violations or other legal situations involving arrests or convictions under penalty of license suspension or revocation.

Pilots are also subject to random tests for drugs and alcohol before and after flights.

This medical and personal scrutiny is definitely an intrusion into a pilot's personal life, but the added layer of safety and reliability for the air travel industry justifies the sacrifice pilots must make. We all accept that the sacrifice goes with the territory.

Face it: from the first day a pilot sets foot into an airline cockpit, we are obsessive about procedures, best practices, crew function, the optimum operation, limits and procedures for our jet, and always, the safety of our flights. We forfeit privacy to the FAA physical every six months, we agree to countless, relentless tests and evaluations, we accept unprecedented scrutiny of every aspect of our professional and even personal lives, for the privilege (it truly is) of flying you wherever you want to go—safely. And we willingly re-prove that to the FAA and our airline every nine months.

That's who's in your cockpit, how they got there, and

how they stay there.

Quick Reference Summary

- Pilots hired by major airlines have extensive flight hours and experience.
- Pilots are constantly tested and evaluated.
- Recurrent training and evaluation is all or nothing: a pilot demonstrates proficiency or is grounded.
- Pilots come from many different backgrounds and career paths, but the common denominator is experience and competence.
- Standardization is the universal synchronization of pilot duties within a carrier—we're all the same, procedurally.
- Perfect procedural and technical function is demanded of pilots—and by pilots. We are hopelessly obsessive about that.
- Pilots are subjected to recurring FAA medical evaluations, plus drug and alcohol screening..

4. YOUR AMAZING AIRCRAFT

In my studies at the USC Flight Safety and Accident Investigation Center, I was astonished to discover the incredibly stringent engineering standards that aircraft designers must meet.

Without getting lost in the mathematical and engineering jungle, here's a thumbnail design sketch. Aircraft manufacturers were given design standards to meet that basically derived a "load[1]" limit the aircraft must withstand in normal flight. To that they added a generous margin and called that the "limit load factor:" the aircraft must withstand this force without suffering any damage or distortion of the structure or flight controls. To that increased margin they again added an additional percentage of force the jet must be able to sustain without experiencing structural failure and that is called the ultimate load factor.

To put limit and ultimate load factors into perspective, those forces are beyond that ever experienced by an airliner in flight and quite frankly, approach the limits of human ability to tolerate such forces. In other words, the strength

[1] In laymen's terms, "load factor" refers to the number of G's, or the force of gravity, the aircraft must be able to tolerate.

envelope is way beyond the endurance of our "2 mile per hour man." That means your remarkable aircraft is built to superhuman strength standards and will tolerate external forces in flight and even on landing that will protect you well beyond any forces you could possibly encounter in flight.

The next tier of wonder is how aircraft designers maintain Sherman-tank strength standards in a vehicle light enough to fly not only smoothly but also economically and in terms of thrust required to sustain flight, efficiently. This is achieved through the ongoing evolution of composite materials that are lightweight but even stronger than older, heavier metals, and advanced engine technology that has produced powerful, lightweight and efficient engines.

This is once again part of the "aviation learning curve" that is the driving force behind commercial aviation: new technology, advanced materials both metal and composite, that are lighter and stronger than in decades past.

Aircraft manufacturers continue to improve designs, producing safer, stronger, more efficient airliners year over year. I'm often asked my preference between the two largest commercial airliner aircraft manufacturers, Boeing and Airbus. I honestly believe both manufacturers produce outstanding, safe, and capable airliners, though I'm a lifelong Boeing pilot at heart. That said, one of the most capable and naturally talented airline pilots I know—my son—flies an Airbus. They're both great aircraft.

Your jet is not only strong—it's very, very smart. Let's start with an area you may not have considered: self-diagnostics. Intercepting systems faults before they can even occur is not only essential to aircraft reliability, it's a huge safety boost for everyone aboard. Sensors constantly monitor aircraft systems and data-link the information to our airline's maintenance and engineering headquarters for tracking and analysis.

The art of data analysis and trend prediction has evolved to the point where a high percentage of both hardware and software failures are uncovered and prevented before they occur. This is particularly true and valuable for aircraft engines: dozens of key parameters are recorded and analyzed. Years of trend data have yielded valid predictive maintenance cues that allow engine reliability to be nearly perfect because latent deficiencies are identified and replaced before there's a failure.

The data transmitted for analysis isn't only about aircraft systems, but rather, the monitored and analyzed data includes every aspect of how the aircraft was configured and flown by the pilots.

Basically, Big Brother monitors and analyzes everything pilots do. If any maneuver, configuration, or procedure is improper or sub-standard, I expect to hear about it. Even though we're the ones being closely monitored, pilots led the way in this valuable safety initiative: we already knew we were held to a very high standard, but we hold ourselves to that standard anyway.

That's a huge liability for pilots: imagine the Highway Patrol monitoring your car through data-linked telemetry, micro-analyzing every move you made on your drive then calling you at home about anything non-standard you did on the road *every single mile you drive*. But pilot unions agreed to this quality assurance monitoring, analysis and reporting system to provide yet another layer of safety monitoring that improves air travel for all.

Unlike your car, the aircraft is gutted on a regularly scheduled basis and practically dismantled to check, test and certify every major system even though nothing has actually gone wrong. But that's the industry safety standard—such checks are mandatory, based on flight hours.

It's not just eyeballs checking, either: the science of "Non Destructive Inspection," or NDI as we call it, has advanced along the aviation learning curve to yield analytic tools like magnetic resonance imaging to detect early signs of metallurgy anomalies; other inspection methods include florescent radiant and eddy current tracking, searching for any weakness in structural components which are either strengthened or replaced.

I could go on about the analysis and maintenance, but let's shift focus to other parts of your aircraft's brain. Navigation systems now are so accurate with the integration of Global Positioning and laser platform Inertial Reference Units that we can fly a departure, a route, an arrival and an approach to within a tolerance measured in feet.

Instrumentation used to be basically a report from rudimentary analog pressure and temperature sensing equipment, which is still on board as a backup, but our primary flight instrumentation if computer-corrected for minute accuracy on a scale undreamed of even twenty years ago. This allows for more reliable vertical separation of airliners because each one is very accurately positioned at their flight level.

My Boeing jet takes that very accurate, detailed information a step further, projecting the essential flight information from our flight instrumentation and navigation systems onto the glass in front of my face so I never have to even look down at the instrument displays while I'm flying an approach.

I like to call this "Head Up Display" (HUD) my "pilot cyborg vision" because even with near zero visibility in bad weather, I can see the runway to land safely because it's outline is projected for me on the glass.

Boeing and some other aircraft manufacturers have been proactive about one other important safety innovation. The reality of most airline accidents is the potentially incendiary combination of fuel tank vapors and an ignition source. On my Boeing jet, a nitrogen generator steadily fills each emptying fuel tank with nitrogen gas which prevents combustion of fuel and vapors, even with an ignition source. That's called "inerting" the fuel tanks and eliminating this risk for all aboard.

I'll explain some other cosmic capabilities we have on board thanks to ever-advancing technology that adds additional protection against weather, terrain and other aircraft later. But one last point: all of these systems are expensive to design, engineer and deploy, but *safety, not cost is the dominant force in airline operations.*

Every commercial airline is a business with a bottom line and I've seen my airline go through desperate financial straits as well boom times of high profits. In the worst of times, we suffer (furloughs, pay cuts, lost retirements) but even in the leanest times, *safety has always been the number one priority and our standards have never been lowered, period.* That's the nature of the airline industry and the government agencies that regulate it—and we wouldn't have it any other way.

Quick Reference Summary

- Your airliner is built to super-human standards of strength and durability.
- Every airliner undergoes recurring maintenance teardown, inspection and analysis to ensure safe operation.
- High tech navigation and positioning systems allow for precise altitude separation from other aircraft.
- Telemetry from your aircraft in flight is gathered and analyzed to intercept systems faults before they can even occur in flight.
- Every maneuver your jet makes is recorded, cached and analyzed to assure conformance with standard operating procedures.
- Innovative safety systems such as "fuel tank inerting" increases your safety in flight.

5. SCARY STUFF

I once found myself plunging straight down from a couple thousand feet, looking up at the tangled mess that was supposed to be my open parachute. I shook the risers like the reins of a stagecoach, hoping to dislodge the sleeve covering my parachute, but it was no use.

Though the smaller drogue chute had pulled the sleeved chute out of the pack properly, a tiny bit of the main chute had poked out of the top of the sleeve and the hundred mile an hour slipstream had inflated a basketball-sized blob of my main chute out the top. It was never going to open.

I looked down and began to distinguish smaller features on the ground, like fences and even some cows who seemed unconcerned. Seeing them rushing up at me I realized I'd spent too much time trying to unsnag my main chute so I had no time left to release it before deploying my reserve chute. That added a high probability that my reserve chute would simply tangle with the flapping, snagged main and I might land on a cow.

I hugged the reserve chute pack tightly, pulled the ripcord and tossed it away. Then I grabbed the reserve silk with both hands and, as I'd been trained in the event of such a streamer as I had flapping above, I threw it downward as hard as I could. I closed my eyes, not wanting to know whether it had tangled with the streamered main or opened—I figured I'd find out soon enough.

The reserve was anchored chest high on my parachute harness and it opened so hard, with so much force that I'd swear my bootheels hit the back of my helmet (nobody warns you about that) yet that was good news: it opened. I'd live.

That, to me, was scary. But, everyone has their own threshold of "scary," and understanding the risks and remedies helps ratchet the anxiety down to a manageable level.

For me, that meant borrowing another parachute and climbing right back aboard the jump plane before I could let fear overinflate itself and stand in my way. For you, that might mean facing down your own fears and getting aboard a jet and flying.

To help, here is, in no particular order, a list of air travel concerns that many fearful flyers have told me they dread, and the reality behind the issue:

--Midair Collision: Let's go back to the well-matured aviation learning curve that is the airline industry. The potential for traffic conflict drove the development of the "Traffic Collision Avoidance System," or TCAS.

The system takes input from aircraft identification signals transmitted by other aircraft and constantly analyzes the geometry of closure, if any occurs. If such closure does develop, the systems sends both aircraft avoidance guidance—not just aural instructions, which it does, but also avoidance symbology on our primary flight display to resolve the conflict and display a clear path—even if one pilot never sees the other.

And let me add an important point: not only was this vital safety layer developed—it was *mandated*, required on all airliners. These systems are expensive to install and maintain, but vital and FAA enforcement assures that they are included on all airliners regardless of cost.

Your car dealer may offer you safety options such as a backup camera or a lane drift sensor—but airlines *must* comply with safety orders, and they all do so willingly and without hesitation. In fact, my airline leaps at the opportunity to make our jets safer.

--Hitting a Mountain: In the late nineties, a mountain crash drove the development of the "Enhanced Ground Proximity Warning System," or EGPWS. This warning system is integrated with the aircraft's instrumentation and navigation computers: it knows where it is at all times—and where all the obstacles in our path are. At the first sign of any closure with terrain or manmade obstacles, aural warnings alert the pilots and as with traffic conflicts, escape symbology appears on pilots' flight displays.

This system is mandatory on all airliners and my airline goes a step further: the FAA may allow the system to be inoperative pending repairs for a set period of time, but my airline takes the uncompromising safety position that says ALWAYS. You'll never fly on one of our jets while the system is temporarily inoperative pending repair.

--Windshear: All airline pilots have a healthy respect for windshear, and that's another area in which advanced aircraft technology has developed great preventative assets. We have aboard the most modern jets—my airline's entire fleet—a Windshear detection And Guidance System," or "WAGS" for short.

This early warning system is integrated with our advanced, solid state radar, air data computers and our flight displays. The on-board radar has its own Global Positioning Satellite (GPS) system and knows where it is at all times. It knows which ground features to screen out and which weather returns to monitor and analyze. The software detects and actually predicts windshear based on Doppler analysis *before* it even occurs. If the radar isn't selected on the pilots' displays, it pops up automatically, along with aural warnings and symbology on the nav displays delineating a clear and safe escape path, just like the TCAS and EGPWS.

Pilots practice escape maneuvers annually in very realistic full motion simulators. We've all learned a very healthy respect for windshear, and to employ advanced tools like WAGs to detect and avoid windshear or if necessary, to escape. Once again, we've got you covered.

--Engine Fire: We have immediate action procedures in case any of the myriad detectors around the engines reports an overheat or fire. Cockpit controls allow us to instantly cut off fuel not only at the engine itself, but also at the fuel tank as well in case the engine fuel shutoff valve is damaged.

We also have a fire suppression system with a secondary backup to fight any engine fire and the reality is, without combustibles (oil and hydraulic fluid are cut off too), there really can be no fire sustained. And an insider, from experience tip: our 200 to 500 mile-per-hour slipstream does a pretty good job of actually blowing out the flames, especially once there are no more combustion sources. Monitoring and detection is instant and continuous, remediation immediate.

--Engine Failure on Takeoff: All of our takeoffs are planned with that potential as the premise. Based on many performance factors, we calculate the maximum speed we can attain and still stop in the remaining runway, as well as the minimum speed we must attain in order to successfully accelerate to takeoff speed on one engine—if and only if we're beyond the stopping distance required.

So, to sort that out, on every takeoff we have the option of stopping or taking off after an engine failure, whichever is safest. Single engine flight is well within the capability of our jet—in fact, it's a design requirement. We practice both discontinued and continued takeoffs as well as single engine approaches and landings exhaustively every year. We're completely safe with both options. In my airline career thus far, I've landed four MD-80 aircraft single engine and to be honest, it's actually smooth, safe—and easier than the annual training we get in single-engine landings.

--Turbulence: It may help to recognize the air we fly in as the fluid it is, which makes it subject to currents, eddies and waves. Like any vessel traversing those disruptive effects, there will be some bumpiness aboard. The choppiness may startle you, given that we're aloft, in the same way railroad tracks under your car's tires will surprise you if you weren't aware of them. But, the result is the same—a little shaking, but no damage or ill effects (go back to Chapter 4, "Your Amazing Jet," to review the design strength of your airframe) beyond a bit of vibration.

Even so, we of course have many layers of information and some new technology to avoid turbulence.

Our latest model on-board radar has an analytical capability that uses Doppler technology to predict turbulence and the movement trend of the turbulence it detects. My airline has a fleet of over 500 jets flying 75,000 flights each month. Most of those jets automatically report choppy rides via data link to our headquarters and so we have quite an active and accurate view of which routes and altitudes to avoid and by contrast, which generate no reports and are therefore smooth—then we route our flights that way.

Air traffic controllers keep us posted on the rides reported ahead of us by aircraft along our route.

We can and will change our altitude or alter our route to find the smoothest air possible. So, when you feel some chop in the aircraft cabin, you can be confident that up front, we're working to find the smoothest air possible. Even so—*always keep your seatbelt fastened when seated.*

--Falling Out of the Sky: This concern is both common—and baseless. Some worry that if both engines were to stop operating in flight, the aircraft would "plummet to the earth," but nothing could be further from the truth. The reality is, if both engines stopped running (has not happened, but let's speculate) we'd simply lower the nose slightly to descend gently at "best drift-down speed," which is the best lift speed. The rule of thumb is we can glide gently a mile for every three thousand feet of altitude above the terrain. So, cruising at 40,000 feet, pilots have a glide range of about 120 miles to effect restart or find a suitable runway. Yes, a jet can easily be glided to a safe landing.

Here's a bit of insider pilot knowledge: with today's advanced jetliners and high lift wings, pilots have to plan descents well ahead of time and start descent early because these wings don't like to descend—or slow down. That's a wonderful asset you can keep in the back of your mind.

--Lightning Strikes: In the air, there's no risk to the aircraft or anyone on board. Lightning may attach itself to the metal skin of an airframe, but then it is safely conducted back into the atmosphere by static wicks on the wings and tail with no effect on aircraft systems. Yes, it can be startling—once I saw a bolt as thick as my arm reach out of the clouds straight ahead and attach itself to the radome with a tremendous bang. My copilot and I exchanged sheepish glances afterward, having drawn our legs up instinctively as if it made a difference. But of course the was virtually no effect on the aircraft.

On the ground, everyone aboard is safe but ground crews can be injured if they're in contact with the metal skin of the plane or if lightning strikes close by, so the ramp will be closed when lightning is within striking range as determined by the airport managers.

--Hitting a Bird: Usually, it's not a problem, just a mess. Once we hit a fairly large bird smack in the middle of my windshield on climb-out from Pittsburgh. The guts smeared across my window, then froze at altitude (temp is usually below -50 C) so I got to look at them for a couple of hours until they thawed on approach and slid off. I still managed to eat my lunch (great deli sandwiches in the Pittsburgh airport) regardless.

I've also had instances where an engine has ingested a bird on approach. On one such occasion, I went down to the ramp to look at the engine with the maintenance techs who'd give it a thorough inspection. There were just a few feathers and remains on the fan blades but I have to admit, the smell of rotisserie chicken from the engine roasting the poor bird actually made me hungry.

But all this is to say, it's not typically a serious problem, which is the reason the "Miracle on the Hudson" is so remarkable. It just doesn't cause much trouble, and even the Sully flight onto the Hudson resulted in no injuries or worse.

These issues are by no means the only things some

31

passengers worry about. You can share your concerns with me through my blog (JetHead.Wordpress.com) where a contact form is in the "About" section. Let me know and I'll address other issues in future editions.

Meanwhile, rest assured: we are ready, willing and able to deal with all challenges on the ground or in the air.

Quick Reference Summary

- The aviation learning curve has driven engineers to design and airlines to deploy sophisticated warning and detection systems for collision, terrain and severe weather avoidance, and they are mandatory on all major airlines' aircraft.
- Pilots are trained to detect and eliminate threats such as windshear and terrain contact and have immediate procedures to deal with every issue.
- Modern airliners are designed to fly safely on one engine, and all takeoffs are designed to be either stopped safely on the runway or flown safely to a single-engine landing, and pilots are extensively trained for both options.
- Lightning seldom if ever causes any problems for an aircraft in flight or on the ground.
- Engine fires are quickly detected and swiftly dealt with through suppression systems.
- Turbulence can be startling, but seldom causes more than just that (review Chapter 4) and pilots have technology and information that will minimize your flight's exposure to such bumps. When the ride gets choppy, rest assured that they're looking for a smoother route and altitude.
- When you pack your own parachute before skydiving, you should be really, really careful so you don't land on an unsuspecting cow or worse.

6. GET UP OFFA THAT THING

Sorry-not sorry: I'm a big James Brown fan. Go ahead, download that song and play it now. You're going to need it.

James Brown was nothing if not a man of action, which is the dividing line between "wanting to" and actually "doing it." That's the great divide that puts you back into a parachute harness leaping out the door of a jump plane, or resigned to an earthbound life for good.

That's what lets you fly with one hand and drop your oxygen mask to use a barf bag with the other (I always made sure I was on "hot mike" so the instructor pilot had to listen) during early aerobatics. The alternative is a groundling life I wouldn't live.

That's what gets you out of your head and onto a very safe, sophisticated and professionally flown jet, going to where you always wanted to go.

So now is the time to Get Up Offa That Thing (did you download it yet? Do—and turn it up) and make your way into the sky.

There's much you can do to take control of your air travel both physiologically and psychologically. Let's start with the latter. Some fearful flyers have been kind enough to share with me a coping technique that makes a lot of sense: track your flight a week to two beforehand. That is, use any one of the many flight tracker smart phone or tablet applications that allow you to track your flight several days running to see for yourself that a) it's pretty routine, and b) what you can expect as far as timing and recurrent delays— or, more likely, your flight runs early or at least smoothly.

The Godfather of Soul

Nothing bad ever happens to the flight, which is just scheduled air service, plain vanilla, like thousands of other flights that day and like you can expect on your flight day.

Reinforce the objective considerations in this book (flip through the bullet points—go back and read in detail when you find specifics that helped you) which are designed to fill the vacuum of "unknown" with the much less ominous reality of facts: your jet, your crew, your flight—all designed and committed to take care of you.

My favorite diversion technique for long flights[2] derives from a psychological technique that has helped me finish nine 26.2 marathons: I set a countdown timer on my watch (most smartphones have them as well) for the anticipated duration of my run or flight. I resist looking at the countdown timer "time remaining" display until well into the flight. Then, it's a real morale booster to see how

[2] I've always hated deadheading, crammed into a passenger seat, bored to death. Then, scrolling through the inflight movie streaming options, I find "Goodfellas"…

much the time has diminished and how comparatively little is left. Once you reach the halfway point and there's left only a fraction of the initial challenge which is a great morale booster: *you've got this.*

This second technique brings up a powerful point you need to remember: *the flight time is finite.* Start running your flight time countdown timer in routine, ordinary life. The flight time is not that long, really, is it?

My daughter used to be impatient about travel, asking how long will the flight be. I'd answer in terms she could understand: two (or three, whatever it was) of her favorite half-hour TV shows. She could relate to that, to the feel and duration. Then she could envision herself in that travel period but more importantly, beyond.

So, for you: how many feature film running times? Or athletic events (3 hour college football broadcasts? MLB games?) could transpire during the allotted flight time? Are those time segments really indefinite? Intolerable? I even project ahead like that for my annual flight evaluations, thinking back a day—then forward: tomorrow at this time I will be successfully complete, and it's really not that far away.

The paralyzing fear of being aboard and aloft can be lessened by realizing it's temporary and, by comparison with other everyday time segments you routinely tolerate, it's not really all that significant. Perspective is key, and that asset is easily within your grasp if you choose to focus on meaningful comparisons.

Once you successfully focus on perspective, try moving beyond the inflight interval to your destination time. The time there will be much, much longer than the flight time you're waiting out enroute. What will you do after you arrive? What experiences are you anticipating after successfully tolerating air travel to get there?

For me, often that means home, a worthy reward for a traveler, especially a flight crewmember so often on the road. It can be that too for you, home, after a long trip. But the point is, you must focus on the reality that the flight is the exception and the destination the rule.

Since you're committed to "get up offa your thing," it's vital to go a step further, now that we've covered some basics. Beyond just tracking your flight and watching how it runs smoothly every day, let's get ready for your flight itself with some more technology. See this for what it is: you, acting, taking action, regarding your flight. *You are not simply acted upon*—rather, you're taking control of an important aspect of your flight: information.

First, your seat selection for your flight. The most stable place on any aircraft is at the center of gravity, usually right over the wings. That's the point around which every motion in yaw or pitch will be felt the least, because just like the hub of a bicycle wheel compared to the tire, that's where the radius of motion is the smallest, hence the least motion and the smoothest ride.

If you're selecting your own seat on-line, refer to the aircraft diagrams the reservation site offers, showing the aircraft's seating arrangement. Take charge of your destiny—select a seat in the center of the cabin, over the wings. If you're using a travel agent or a live phone contact, specify that you want to reserve a seat in the center of the cabin.

The seats very far aft in the cabin swing and pitch the most because they are the farthest from the center of gravity. Avoid those seats.

You, enjoying a refreshing beverage, re-reading this book in flight.

The aircraft center of gravity, over the wings, where you wisely reserved a seat knowing that's where the ride is smoothest.

The seats right over the wing often are near an over-wing emergency exit. If that increases your stress, simply book a seat ahead of or behind the emergency exit row. If you are reassured by sitting near an over-wing emergency exit—you'll be the first one safely evacuated from the aircraft if need be—then definitely book the exit row seat. Also, be aware that some exit row seats do not recline or recline only a little, but in my mind that's more than compensated for by the extra legroom those exits rows have.

Again, take charge of this seat selection detail, which can also rightfully be seen as "smoothness selection:" *you* are in control of this.

A final word about seats: be sure you have *assigned seats* before you conclude your on-line or by phone reservations. This is important because at the airport, if you do not have paper boarding passes or electronic records indicating a seat assignment, you are not assured of seating where you'd planned to sit.

Another asset that most travelers don't consider is the advantage of flying early in the day. The air is smoother before the sun has time to heat things up, creating thermals and convection. But as importantly, the airport is less crowded. Why? Because few connecting flights have arrived early in the day compared to later on. That means less people in the airport and in many cases, on planes.

You also will probably not have to wait for your outbound plane to arrive, avoiding any delays the inbound flight may have experienced. More often, your aircraft parked at your departure the night before and all maintenance and preflight preparation has been done. Your crew, too, will be originating and not susceptible running out of legality due to delays.

Later in the day, aircraft may be delayed inbound, crews can misconnect and connecting passengers may add additional crowding to the terminal and gate. If you have a choice, fly early.

There are more ways to empower yourself. Download the smartphone application for your particular airline or if there's more than one carrier involved, download as many as are necessary. If you don't need them after your trip, they're easily deleted but if you'd like to control your own destiny, get them now.

Most have a set-up option to allow them to send you "push" notifications if you enable the function. *Do enable the function* so you will receive live updates on your departure and arrival gates, your baggage claim area, delays and cancellations. Don't wait to be told, don't search out monitors in the airport—push notifications bring all of that information to you.

At the very least, have your flight number handy and if nothing else, you can Google your flight: "AA flight 349," enter, will yield the latest information instantly. The airline's app will take the guesswork out of flight numbers and itineraries—yours will be preloaded and information will flow to you. But if all else fails, just Google your flight number.

This isn't a "fear of flying" consideration but rather a general air travel issue: passengers wander about looking for their gate in the terminal. When they ask a crewmember for help, they typically don't even know their flight number. At best, we might get "the San Francisco flight." Problem is, there may be a half dozen flights to any city in a given day.

This is where you can and should move to the head of the class: know your flight number and, to make it easy, get your airline's app and use it. Keep your phone on in the terminal and on board your flight when allowed. Check for those push notifications and beat the crowd to the gate, the new gate, and with some apps, you'll be rebooked on a new flight if yours cancels.

You're not done with your psychological groundwork yet. To take control of your destiny, to enable yourself to act efficiently and effectively in this air travel challenge you're undertaking, there's one more piece of knowledge you can easily own: every major airport has a website with maps depicting terminal layout, location of key services, and transportation options. Pore over these like a general planning an assault, because that's exactly what you're doing—you want to know how the gates, terminals, and baggage claim are laid out. If you're renting a car, you need to know where to find your rental agency; if there's ground transportation involved, you must be able to find it.

Search now, study, understand the terminals you'll need to traverse. Knowledge is power in all things, but especially in air travel. "The unknown" that contributes to your reluctance to travel by air can be drastically reduced if you plan your own airport invasion beforehand.

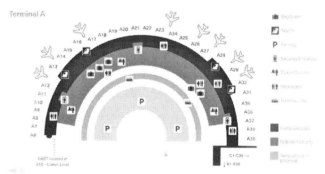

One final option you may choose in the United States is either Global Entry or TSA Pre-Check. There is a fee involved for both, so I recommend Global Entry (Search for US Customs-Global Entry) because this program will also enroll you in TSA Pre-Check as well as Global Entry for the same fee.

TSA Pre-Check for those who qualify streamlines the airport security screening and will speed you on your way with less disruption. Global Entry will allow you to clear US Customs very quickly via special, modified procedures. Both of these programs, if you qualify, can eliminate layers of stress for you. Again, *you* are in charge: investigate both programs and see if they're valuable for your travel needs.

The second half of your "get up offa" strategy involves physiological preparation, and this is pretty basic. First, be rested and well-hydrated before your flight. That may sound simplistic, but both are important.

First, be rested: stress is easier to handle if you are rested and once the trip begins it's less likely that you'll stay well-rested. That's easy to underestimate but important to consider when you travel: you won't sleep as well, nor get the normal amount of rest you need once you switch time zones and living quarters, whether you're staying with family or elsewhere.

This latter thing—elsewhere—flight crews refer to as "hotel sleep:" it's not the same, there's lots of noise, different bed, different place. Hotel sleep is worth about half a night of home sleep, so anticipate that. Take it easy in the days leading up to your flight if you can.

Hydration is another crucial factor easily overlooked when you travel. Be aware that the humidity on most airliners in flight is extremely low—1% in most cases—and just through respiration alone you can easily become dehydrated, accruing all of the negative effects dehydration brings. So stay hydrated before, during and after your flight and you'll find yourself more capable of handling the flight and post-flight challenges. Remember, too, that alcohol and caffeine contribute to dehydration so avoid alcohol and be sparing with caffeine.

To be specific, bring at least a liter of water aboard—you'll need to get that once you're through security screening either from a concession or a water fountain—and have it within reach in flight. Same goes for calories: bring any type of dry snack that suits you, but have calories within reach because even if there are "buy on board snacks[3]" for sale on your flight, the timing of the service might not match your physiological needs or the time zone in which your body normally functions.

Most of the "buy on board" snacks are very good, in my experience, but depending on how the aircraft is catered and where the flight attendants start their in-flight service, your choice might not be available. Whether in the cockpit or the cabin, I always have some type of emergency ration (usually some type of protein bar) on hand to take care of my own needs.

That brings me to a final point about food and water: go to the TSA website on line to become informed of the most current restrictions on liquids and carry-on items, as well as specifics about the security screening before your flight. The security people themselves point out how much smoother and faster your screening experience will be if you're familiar with the process and restrictions.

---

[3] Most airlines accept only credit or debit cards, no cash.

And one more important factor you should give thought to before your flight: the dress code. Clearly, there is no dress code at the airport or on the airplane[4], but practicality matters for your comfort and safety. First, resort wear is impractical because the temperature on the aircraft may not match the destination you've dressed for. Specifically, resort wear designed for tropical weather will leave you chilled in an aircraft at altitude.

The temperature on-board is controlled mainly from the cockpit, and we get input from the cabin crew about how hot or cold the cabin is. They are working wrapped in layers of polyester so what feels comfortable to them might be too chilly for tropical wear. We keep the working crew happy—so you might not be comfortable in shorts and a T-shirt, but their request for a cooler cabin is what we go by.

And even more practical matter is an evacuation: you'll be out in the elements and shorts and flip flops will not suffice for comfort or safety.

---

[4] Again, Google "passenger shaming:" what people wear to fly in is outrageous and impractical.

Be sure to dress for a long, slightly cool-ish ride that may not match your destination weather. Dress for the flight, not the arrival.

There's a lot for you to consider in this chapter, but all of it is important to your successful air travel experience. So, get up offa that thing, and let's review:

Quick Reference Summary

- Track your flight in the week leading up to your travel. See how it does as far as being on time or delayed. Note that it routinely functions safely.

- Download and set up your airlines application on your smartphone or tablet. Enable push notifications to keep current on gate, baggage claim and on-time status.

- Know your flight information (flight number, destination and connecting cities) and use Google when all else fails to find your gate and flight status.

- Consider "trusted traveler" programs such as Global Entry and TSA Pre-Check if you are eligible and if the program will save you time and stress.

- Study the airport diagrams of the airports you'll traverse during your trip. Know where the basic services that affect your trip (other terminals, baggage claim, car rental, ground transportation) and keep the information accessible (bookmark, print—whatever you prefer).

- Take control of the "are we there yet" question: practice with a countdown timer in everyday life to be familiar with just how finite you flight will be. Relate the interval to other segments of your life to keep the duration in a manageable perspective.

- Use a countdown timer in flight to reinforce your minute by minute progress towards flight completion.

- Focus on destination activities as you make your way through security, on board, and in flight. .
- Carry both water and some type of calories on board.
- Try to be rested before your trip, thereby boosting your ability to handle the routine stress of air travel.
- Avoid alcohol and limit caffeine.
- Download James Brown to psych up for your trip.

7. FLIGHT DAY: YOUR PILOTS

The Great and Powerful Oz didn't want you to notice the mere mortal behind the curtain, but I do. Knowledge is power when it comes to flying and the more you know the more at ease you can be about your flight. We'll look at how your flight day should unfold next. If you're interested, here's a fairly routine day evolves for the typical airline pilot.

I start my flight day with a "look back:" the FAA is concerned with my twelve hours preceding a flight. Did I get enough rest? I'll need to certify that before each flight leg of the day but more importantly, I arrange my life to ensure that I've got a clean look-back. That's partly for the FAA, but mostly for me: I need to be at my best today to faithfully serve over 300 passengers who will put their trust in me. Crew rest is key because the workday will be 10-12 hours.

I don't care for early flights so I don't "bid" them. All flight crew schedules are awarded based on seniority and I have several decades of that, so I get what I want: late morning report times, nine or ten o'clock returns.

Here's something you can do too on your flight day: step outside, feel the air, see the sky, decide what's likely to happen there, because that's where you'll spend your day. I like to think this is what old sea captains did, feeling in their bones what's up with the weather they'll encounter once they sail. After four decades as a pilot, I think I kind of get it. A quiet moment, the feel of the air, the look of the sky. There will be fifteen layers of meteorology and high-tech science ahead at the airport helping flight planners determine our route and fuel requirements, but the morning first feel is probably as valid and definitely essential.

I allow extra time to drive in to the airport, and you should too for the same reason: I don't want this flight day to start with stress. I bid trips that fall outside of rush hour but I still leave extra time for the drive. Relax—we'll be early. And enjoy the secret knowledge as you check out the flags flying or smokestacks blowing and you analyze the wind rather than the taillights like everyone else: we look up because that's where we're going to spend our day.

In the terminal I'm like most people just trying to get by, find my flight and gate, then get aboard. From a crew perspective it often seems like passengers look at us in the terminal like costumed characters at a theme park. In reality, I have a lot of work to do and theater isn't on my list. So, I keep to myself and try to slip by unnoticed. Still, I'll always help four types of people: the very young, the very old, those who don't speak the language, and our military folks. That's it. If you don't know where your gate is, it's because you haven't Googled it. Or written your flight number down. Or acted like a responsible adult and planned ahead as I outlined in the last chapter.

I'll walk down to airline flight operations and visit with pilot and flight attendant friends who are also reporting for flights. Used to be flight crews met in flight ops before a trip so the captain could discuss weather charts and possible route considerations with his copilot and crew. But now, everything is digital and I can get the most current weather and flight planning information on my smart phone or uploaded to my company-issued tablet on board the jet. I prefer this new, paperless cockpit and we can discuss everything that matters on board.

By the time I get to the airport, Flight Operations and Dispatch has figured the best routing given the current winds and enroute weather and they've filed a flight plan and decided on how much fuel we'll need. I'll take another look at both the weather and the route, then figure in what I know to be the typical delays or problems I know from experience and then I'll decide if I agree with the planned route and fuel.

If my gut feel is that we'll need more fuel, I'll call our flight's dispatcher at our airline operations center and tell them I want more. In over twenty-six years as captain I've never had any answer back other than "Sure—how much?"

Headed for the gate, I try to be invisible. I'm not a fan of "air travel theater," glad-handing and posing. I like to be single minded about getting to altitude without screwing anything up or bending any metal. I'm not on vacation or a pleasure cruise—it's my responsibility to orchestrate a safe flight.

I usually arrive at the departure gate before the rest of

the crew does. I like to get there an hour prior if possible so that I can stow my flight gear without having to squeeze past everyone from cabin cleaners to caterers who swarm over the jet between flights. I check the aircraft's maintenance logbook, which I can also do from my phone or tablet, but I like to verify that there are no paper maintenance entries open that might not have made it into the digital record.

I check the battery voltage to be sure that vital back up electrical source is fully charged, then I start both navigation systems and let them align. That's it—time for the captain to head back into the terminal to stay out of everyone else's way: the first officer has a lot of checks and set-up items to do, the cabin crew is busy with their preflight duties and my goal is to let everyone do their job—they all know what they're doing—and stay out of their hair.

My strategic planning includes buying a cup of coffee to-go at about twenty minutes prior to pushback. That's the magic time interval that will ensure the coffee remains hot so I can drink it on climb out after takeoff. A simple pleasure.

I slip into the cockpit and set up all my stuff—tablet, flight plan and weather radar depiction, the departure plan, my headset and communications panel.

As in the terminal, I don't do "airline theater," standing in the cockpit doorway mugging for the marketing department. I prefer to sustain the singular focus and let my first officer see that: we're about the mission here. As I mentioned earlier, centripetal thinking: we're concentrating on wrapping this task in several perfect procedural layers and executing it perfectly. Anything else is a distraction.

I *will* greet some very special passengers if I know they're on board: animals being shipped in the cargo compartment. If there's time, I'll ask the flight attendants for a liter of bottled water and go down to the ramp. Cats seem oblivious but dogs are often scared and befuddled. The ramp is subjected to extremes of noise, weather and temperature and in my opinion, that's no place for a pet. The least I can do is offer a reassuring word, a friendly hand and a water dish refill before the cargo door is closed. It's the right thing to do.

I feel it's also the captain's job to take a broad view of the final minutes before pushback. It's important for someone to stand aside from whatever last minute rush is going on (slow down, folks, no awards for rushing) and look at the big picture: it's a minor delay, relax. Take a deep breath and settle down. We'll go when we're ready, when all the requirements are met.

TMI Alert

From this narrative point you might find the details to be "Too Much Information" and if so, skip past this section. I only offer this part for some flyers who will be reassured by the details. If the "behind the cockpit door" perspective raises your anxiety, simply skip to the next chapter.

I keep a side-eye on my First Officer, noting whether he or she seems busy and if so, I stay quiet. When things seem quiet, they're likely caught up and that's when I'll call for a checklist. But even that will be *sotto voce*: "Shall we read 'em?" or "How about we check the route?" A suggestion, an option. Yes, it needs to be accomplished, but no need to be a task master. And, I've learned in 26+ years as captain, if I'm laid back, the FO will be too. I like that best.

So, we go through all of our required cockpit checks in a "challenge and response" format—the FO reads the check, I verify the required action has been done. Example: Challenge: "pressurization."
Response: [I check the panel to be sure the configuration of valves is correct, the planned altitude set, the system in auto mode] "Auto and set."

So, the FO has set the system up accurately and I've checked and verified the set-up and confirmed the configuration.

So it goes through each system and procedure. The binary aspect is the strength of flight operations: accomplish the required task, verify, confirm. There are standard challenges read exactly off a checklist and standard responses given. That's a "litany," as we call it, and it's as rigid as an old school Mass. That's part of its strength: standardization, consistency, thoroughness.

Finally, when all checklists have been accomplished, we're ready for pushback. When the cabin is secure ("seated and stowed, cabin ready" is the flight attendants' cue to me that they're ready) I call the ground crew via headset. The ground crew chief on the ramp is on headset and we talk via the flight interphone. He tells me when the ground crew is clear and ready for pushback.

I call for the "Just Prior" checklist; again we verify a litany of tasks by a challenge and response exchange. I'm only listening to the crew chief in my headset while the FO communicates with ramp control in the airline ramp tower, requesting clearance for pushback. I only listen to the crew chief because it's vital that we focus our full attention on the aircraft under tow (a tug pushes us back) and I need instant focus and response to the chief as we maneuver our 130 foot wide, 135 foot long footprint among a variety of other aircraft and ground vehicles.

We usually are cleared to start engines as we push back, so I call for that portion of the checklist. The FO starts the right engine when we're cleared. When we're pushed to the correct position, I call for the left engine to be started. I'm always very careful about this because a running jet engine even at idle power will suck a person right off their feet and into the engine if they're within ten feet of the intake. The crew chief signals me when they're all safely clear.

Finally, after the tug is disconnected and the interphone door closed, the chief holds up a red streamer that has the steering pin on it, showing me that our steering has been enabled now that the tug is disconnected. We exchange salutes and I tell the FO, "I have a salute," which means we're cleared to taxi.

I make sure I visually check that the ground crew is clear. The FO and I both clear left and right, then I join the FO on the ramp or ground frequency for taxi instructions.

This is where we go to "sterile cockpit:" no extraneous, non-essential talk. For example: "How 'bout them Cowboys" is forbidden and, in my mind, annoying— we're concentrating on not missing any important instructions or details as we roll a seventy ton jet across the spaghetti bowl of taxiways. But, "If you miss this taxiway after you exit the runway you have to go to the end because the other taxiway is closed" is fair game—it's about the mission.

I like things quiet in the cockpit. There's no need for over-elaborating—the standard verbiage will do just fine. That's probably my military flying background: in the cockpit and on the radio, you say what needs to be said and then shut up. That reduces clutter on a crowded radio frequency and reduces distraction in the cockpit. Hollywood depictions of airline crews typically includes a lot of conversational crap and "standbys" and "rogers," but that's mostly fiction. And I'm more likely to say "okie-doke" than "roger" just because "roger" sounds so cliché.

As we taxi to the runway, our flight ops people will uplink our final weight and balance data to our on-board printer. This is the last piece of the puzzle we need to fine-tune our takeoff performance plan.

The FO updates the onboard data, then briefs me on the aircraft weight details, the current winds and the required power settings.

I have before me the planned takeoff weight and I compare that to the uplinked weight, then compare that with the weight and target thrusts settings displayed by our aircrafts Flight Management Systems (FMS). If there's any discrepancy, we resolve that before takeoff.

There's typically a line of jets (I call it "the aluminum conga line") lumbering awkwardly to the runway and we take our spot in the taxi stream, waiting for our turn for takeoff. When ground control gives us any taxi instructions, I interject "Got it" before the FO can even answer just to let him know I'm clear on what we need to do. If it's a major restriction, I'll repeat it aloud so the FO can confirm: "Holding short of runway five," for example.

So it goes—quietly, if I have my taciturn way—as we approach the runway. When we are at last cleared onto the runway there are final checklist items to be called out and responded to. Then I reiterate the target takeoff power setting, give the winds and runway a quick check, the radar too if clear path is necessary.

Once cleared for takeoff, I push the power up to approximately 40% of takeoff power, let the indications stabilize, then I press the autothrottle button that moves them forward to takeoff power, I hack the chronometer so I can keep track of elapsed time—then we roll.

When we accelerate through 80 knots, the FO calls "80" so we can cross-check that our airspeed indicators match. I also glance down at both sets of engine instruments to be sure all is normal while we're still below maximum takeoff abort speed.

The aircraft verbally announces V1, the takeoff decision speed: beyond V1, we're committed to flight. V1 is a relief to me: I'm a pilot, I can fly anything and I'd rather fly even a problem-stricken jet than wrangle a seventy-ton tricycle to a stop on the runway.

At the proper speed, the FO calls "rotate" and I ease the control column back and she flies off the ground. I'm careful to not raise the nose too much too fast because the fuselage is so long that we need altitude clearance for the tail above the runway before I set climb pitch.

Then we're off. I love the feel of potential before we roll, I live the graceful ease of the jet after we're off the ground. We both verify navigation modes and track, then it's all about the charted headings, altitudes, speeds and track as we climb to cruise altitude. My coffee in one hand, the other hand-flying the jet: that's one of life's simple pleasures.

The "shut up" period extends to ten thousand feet, which is also where we lower the nose slightly and accelerate to climb speed and eventually, cruise Mach.

This takeoff process is the same when the FO is making the takeoff, with me in the backup role. We ease our way up to cruise altitude, monitoring all vital systems as we go.

That's the TMI account of taxi out and takeoff. And that concludes the **TMI Alert**, and everyone can rejoin here for the:

Quick Reference Summary

- Rest before a flight is vital if you expect to have enough energy for a demanding flight day.
- Allowing extra travel time to the airport eliminates stress from the outset of a busy day.
- Knowing your key information (flight number and gate) is vital to effective travel.
- I leave other crewmembers to their duties because they all know what they're doing and I don't want to interfere.
- Flight planning starts way before the flight and gets revised and optimized all the way up to takeoff.
- Pilots use the binary of "challenge and response" to verify procedures and configuration.
- The combination of good coffee and a smooth hand-flying jet is one of life's simple pleasures.

8. FLIGHT DAY: YOU

This is the day you've planned, arranged and made choices to enact as a capable passenger: all the psychological and physiological prep to take control of your flight has been done. Today is the payoff for all of your diligent preparation. Honestly, if you've attended to the suggestions in this book thus far, you are going to be way ahead of the other passengers, fully in charge of your flight experience.

Let's walk through the flight day for you so that when that day comes, you can visualize yourself successfully managing the choices and options before you. I'll also highlight some "best practices" travel tips for you that are simple but often overlooked even by more experienced air travelers. These tips willl save you time and effort.

Your "look back" should reflect a decent attempt at rest and hydration. Next, allow extra time to get to the airport. How long do you figure the drive to the airport will take? Add an hour to that. Plan to be through airport security screening at least an hour prior to boarding time— not departure time, *boarding* time, which is even earlier.

It goes without saying that you need to know both the boarding time and the departure time. Write those down, put them into your smart phone—whatever it takes to have this vital information handy. If you've set up the airline app on your smart phone, that info will be at your fingertips.

So, now you have a "leave home" time that is generously and wisely padded to avoid stress before you even get on board your flight.

Here's an example. I live about 35 minutes from my hometown airport if traffic is normal. When I'm flying on vacation with my family, we plan to step out the door three hours prior to our flight's departure. That gives us plenty of time to drive, park and clear security screening. In the typical case, we end up having an hour to kill in the airport, which is the perfect opportunity to sit down at an airport restaurant for whatever mealtime we'll miss because we're in the air.

Even if there's a traffic or parking hassle, we still won't be rushed. And as important, everyone will be hydrated and calorized before we board.

To put the airport experience into a context you can picture, think of a major theme park or athletic venue as people flock to the site. There will be crowds who will be handled *en masse* for entry and traffic flow. There will be all ages and demographics crowding the entry and the terminal. Be ready for a mass-market experience, as a large number of travelers converge in a small space.

Many if not most of your fellow travelers will not have considered the issues we've discussed and will slow down every aspect of your air travel as a result. Here's a conversation I've actually had with a passenger who stopped me in the airport:

> Passenger: Where is the terminal?
> Me: We're in the terminal.
> Passenger: The gate?
> Me: [ready to Google] What is your flight number?
> Passenger: Where is Alaska?

This is the root cause of much of the airport chaos: simple information, easily obtained (flight number) but too often overlooked by passengers before they get to the airport.

Meanwhile, your goal once you arrive at the airport is to find the least crowded security screening checkpoint. If the first line you encounter is crowded, ask the TSA person checking IDs where the nearest, less crowded checkpoint might be. They'll know and can direct you to a less crowded option. If you've studied the airport diagram ahead of time, you'll know if an alternative checkpoint is a possibility. Most major airports have several security checkpoints.

Once you've checked any luggage with the airline, it really doesn't matter what security checkpoint you use as long as you can get to your gate by boarding time. Again, you have to be familiar with the inter-terminal transportation at your airport as well as your boarding time.

If you were able to register for TSA-Precheck, you'll have a more streamlined, less crowded entry experience. If not, anticipate lines, especially at prime travel times.

Important Flight Tip: before you leave home, pack your valuables (jewelry, watch, wallet, keys) in a lockable hand-carry bag that you plan to carry on board. *Do not wear watches, rings or jewelry, nor carry a wallet.* You'll have to remove these items at the security checkpoint and place them in an open container to pass through the security checkpoint scanner. *You will be separated from these items as you pass through the security arch, and they will be vulnerable to theft while they are out of your sight and control.*

Valuables are stolen daily from the screening checkpoint (signs warn that the security screeners are not responsible for lost or stolen items) chaos that is harried passengers trying to collect their valuables and rush to a departure gate. Lock yours in a hand-carried bag and once you've cleared security, find a spot to collect yourself, your group, and your belongings *then* put on watches and jewelry.

To clear security, you need two things in hand: your identification and your boarding pass. The rest needs to be safely locked away in a tamper-resistant bag.

If security screeners need to inspect the bag's contents, fine—they can do so in your presence after you unlock it.

Important Flight Tip: Use the "tag team" approach as you transit security. That is, for two or more people, coordinate your passage. For example, my wife goes through the security arch first, then and only then do I put our items to be screened on the conveyer belt. Then she's already screened and can retrieve all of our property before I go through. That way, someone always has positive contact with our property even if one or the other of us is pulled aside for further screening. At no time are our valuables laying out in the open and vulnerable to theft.

This is essential if you're traveling with children: send and adult through, then the child, then the other adult. That way your child is not alone, out of your reach.

We call the locked hand-carry bag "The Football," after the bag of nuclear launch codes the President of the United States travels with at all times. We keep all of our travel documents, valuables, prescriptions and cash in it and someone has an eyeball on it at all times.

Now, the mystery of gates and flights. During the course of an airport day, each gate will have several flights arrive and depart to various destinations. So, if you arrive at the gate that's currently designated for your flight but the sign shows another flight at the gate, don't panic. Use your airline app or Google to verify that your gate info is correct. If so, just relax: another flight must be scheduled to depart before yours.

What may have happened, however, is a gate change. This isn't a problem as long as you stay aware of such changes (again, the app can send you live updates) and move to the new gate right away.

Passengers often ask why gates change once they're posted. That's simple: if the flight on a particular gate experiences a delay, the flight bound for that gate needs a new gate so that passengers inbound (some continuing on, some not) can get to the terminal. That means a gate change.

This happens less frequently early in the day because many aircraft are originating, meaning, already on the gate. But airline operations are susceptible to inbound delays to air traffic congestion, weather and maintenance. The only way to keep passengers moving from one flight to a connecting flight is to change gate assignments.

Once you're through security screening, here are some unforeseen problems that you may encounter. This isn't to suggest that these problems always happen, but in the interest of knowledge making for a smoother flight experience for you, here are some typical obstacles that you might encounter: For each, the solution is simply, patience: these complications will be worked out.

Possible Complications

Ramp Closure: This means the airport has stopped ramp operations including baggage loading and unloading, aircraft fueling and catering due to a weather condition, typically lightning. Most major airports have a lightning detection system which alerts them when there is the potential for lightning on the ramp. Smaller airports may use the National Weather Service warnings. The important thing is that ground workers are not put at risk.. These delays are only temporary.

Ground Stop: This term means there has been a freeze on departures and arrivals at a particular airport. That is usually due to traffic problems from different causes, but the most typical is weather and second, air traffic overload. A ground stop may also be due to a computer or electrical power failure affecting air traffic control in a certain area. Whatever the cause may be, the intent is—and I think it makes sense—that it's better to hold aircraft on the ground at a departure station rather than have to hold them in the air, waiting for approach clearance.

Weather many miles from the airport can cause a ground stop because arrival routing might be restricted by weather in the terminal area, limiting the arrival paths and as a result, the rate at which approaches can be flown.

If we hold on the gate at our departure airport, you'll be allowed to deplane if you want to. But, be aware, you must take all of your belongings with you if you choose to deplane. It's just another temporary setback—less likely early in the day though.

Wheels Up Time: That's slang for Expect Departure Clearance Time (EDCT), or "edict" as pilots say. This means that your flight has been assigned a spot in the traffic flow to your destination, but the designated takeoff time is after your scheduled departure time. This is typical in the second half of the day (again, fly early) due to the normal buildup of air traffic congestion in certain parts of the airways.

If the EDCT is more than two hours beyond your scheduled departure time, your flight will likely not be boarded until it's within a normal taxi out and takeoff time period so that no one has to sit on a plane for hours.

You may, however, find yourself waiting on the taxiway for an hour or so because you can be kept reasonably comfortable on board for that shorter time period, which works to everyone's advantage: often, EDCTs are shortened or cancelled and the fastest way to your destination is for your flight to be boarded and in line for takeoff. During the delay, I'll keep you informed at least every thirty minutes (a requirement in the US) on the PA of our most current delay status.

Often, too (and this is real insider information) if we're boarded and parked near the runway waiting out an EDCT, I will use my cellphone to call our Ops Center and talk them into calling the FAA Traffic Management Office to see if they can't negotiate a shorter delay or even a release from the EDCT. Often, that works but you have to be out there, ready for takeoff.

Aircraft Out Of Service: Simply means that the jet needs maintenance work that would delay the flight unreasonably, so there'll be another aircraft and gate assigned to the flight.

This may or may not affect your arrival time at your destination depending on when the decision to change aircraft is made. But this situation once again underscores the need for you to have your airline's app on your phone: the same system that alerts me and my crew of an aircraft change via push notification will send you a text advising you of the change and the new gate if you've set the app up.

Awaiting Crew: An unfortunate reality of crew life is that one some days, you have to switch aircraft between flight legs. That's a hassle for us but a potential delay for you if our inbound flight is delayed (if you needed yet one more reason to fly early, here you go) then we may not be aboard your flight at its scheduled departure time. If the delay is seriously long, the airline may protect the downline connections by using a reserve flight crew, but that might take time to do as well.

Crew Duty Limit: The FAA has prudently limited the length of a pilot's on duty period for safety reasons. If your pilots have been on duty near the limit, they may have to be replaced before you can depart. This happens late in the day (sound familiar?) when unforeseen cumulative flight delays push a pilot's duty time past the FAA limit. That's a problem for us, too, often meaning we have to spend the night somewhere when we'd planned to be home, and find our way home the next day. Many passengers seem to get annoyed at this situation, but flight safety is paramount, the FAA rules are intractable and this situation is just something we all have to accept as one of the standards that keeps air travel safe.

Oversold Flight: This means there are more ticketholders for the flight than there are seats on the aircraft. If you have boarding passes with assigned seats, you're all set. This is one reason why I stress that *you must have seat assignments* on your boarding pass or electronic records—otherwise, you will be assigned a seat wherever they can fit you in. If you were counting on a seat near the wings (Remember? The most stable place on board) you might find yourself assigned a seat elsewhere on board.

Regardless, an oversold flight may be an opportunity if your travel plans allow a delay. A major airline will not deny a ticketholder a seat but instead, will simply offer incentives for ticketed travelers to voluntarily give up their seat.

Incentives include travel vouchers good for future fares, plus in some cases, a hotel room, meals and incidentals. Beyond deciding if a later flight will work for you, there's one very vital detail you must see to if you're going to voluntarily give up you seat. That is, *you must insist on an assigned seat* on a specific alternative flight. If that isn't specified, you may find yourself on standby, no seat guaranteed and your travel on hold. *If the compensation offer doesn't include a confirmed seat on a later flight, I wouldn't accept the offer.*

Another bit of insider information: often passengers take the first offer, but if no one does, they'll keep upping the offer until someone does. And be aware that your checked bags will go on to your destination without you, another good reason to keep all of your important items including travel documents and required prescriptions in your hand-carried "football."

Cancelled Flight: This is the airline version of the blue screen of death on your computer. But, don't worry: the airline has sold you a seat and will transport you. This is another reason why you need to have the airline's app working on your phone: many will allow you to find another flight and even rebook—before many passengers even realize the flight is cancelled.

A major airline will accommodate you on another flight, which is why it's important to book your flight with a major airline with many flights available. Regardless, you do have rights as a paying passenger and they may include compensation. The main thing is to ensure your travel as quickly and efficiently as possible. Get the on the airline's app, or immediately dial the airline's reservations number to rebook.

Once you've resolved any of these issues, the next step is boarding the aircraft. Remember, these issues are typically just temporary, requiring both patience and awareness on your part. Stay informed through digital media (announcements in the airport are often difficult to hear) and know your options but basically, sit tight and things will work out.

Your boarding pass may specify a "Group Number" (or letter) which will be called when it's time for you to board. Crowding the gate before your group is called only slows the process down and really, there's no rush: the jetbridge (the corridor from the boarding area to the aircraft) may be either too hot or cold for comfort, so there's no reason to stay there any longer than necessary. The aircraft isn't moving till everyone's seated, no matter what their boarding priority is. Relax until your group is called, then join the line.

Quick Reference Summary

- Be certain that your boarding pass has a seat assignment before your flight day.
- Add at least an hour to your anticipated travel time to the airport to account for unforeseen delays in traffic, parking and in some cases, rental car return.
- Dress for the plane ride, which will likely be colder than you expect. Resort wear is impractical in flight and especially, in an evacuation.
- Pack your jewelry and valuables in a secure hand-carried bag; **do not** place valuables in open bins to go through security screening.
- Keep all essential items (documents, medications, credit cards, valuables) in one hand-carried bag in case you are separated from your luggage enroute or at your destination.

- If traveling with another person, use the "tag team" approach to screening to ensure someone always has positive contact with and control over your valuable.
- Stay connected to your airline's latest flight information via push notifications on your cell phone. Be ready to Google information as well.
- Once beyond the security checkpoint, buy water to carry aboard and grab a bite to eat if you can.
- Be familiar with the potential complications listed in this chapter and be prepared to wait.
- Board only when your group is called to speed the boarding process.

9. IN FLIGHT: WHAT TO EXPECT

I've flown a lot of long-haul, transoceanic flights (longest: fourteen hours) as a pilot and I always found it useful to pace myself in order to whittle down what can seem like a monolithic flight time.

For example, I've flown from DFW to Europe many, many times and that flight time can vary between eight and twelve hours depending on the winds and the destination. So I'd chip away at the total time this way, on an eight hour flight to London. First, I'd throw away the first and last hour, because we'll be fairly busy with takeoff, climb, descent and approach during those periods and they'll fly by rapidly on their own.

Now we're down to six hours, but I can lop off another cockpit hour with dinner: there'll be a fairly elaborate meal service, including appetizers if we haven't pissed-off the flight attendants, and that will take at least an hour, maybe longer. I don't typically eat airplane food if I can bring my own (can't really do that on longer flights) but this gets us down to five hours, the length of an ordinary transcon flight.

Next, I blot out the middle hour. That's another marathon survival technique: at mile eighteen, I take a Zen break: clear my mind of all thoughts of running and effort and concentrate inwardly, on the road, my breathing, pace, resting mentally. In flight, I focus on navigation, fuel flow, systems—never mind the time, just as much of an hour when I can just be a pilot, attentive to the flight and nothing else.

Fill another hour with breakfast, thinking about it and actually eating, shaking off any fatigue, having strong coffee: sometimes the flight attendants double-bag the brew for strength and that's a real eye-opener, especially valuable as we've been awake all night going eastbound. Okay, we're down to three hours and that's actually less than DFW to Boston or Seattle, so no big deal.

You can pretty much toss out the early and late parts of your flight for the same reason: they'll be new and exciting for you. Set your countdown timer as we discussed earlier and be ready to start it just as I do the cockpit chronometer as we begin our takeoff roll. No, it's not vital that either of us do that, but we both want to know "how much longer," don't we? I do.

I described earlier how push-back goes from the cockpit perspective. Here's a summary of what you'll see, hear and feel during the various phases of your flight from your viewpoint in the cabin so you can anticipate them, understand them and be at ease, knowing things are just as they should be.

Your Seat: Whether you're in First Class, Business Class, or Coach, there's just not much personal space, so it's vital that you're disciplined on a couple things. First, "what comes out must go back." That is, take out whatever you need from your hand-carried bag (preferably, "The Football" as we've discussed) but then *put it back when you're finished using it*. That's exactly what I do in the cockpit with my flight gear—if I'm not using it, I'm losing it (you will too) if I don't put it away. There are always notes posted on the flight crew bulletin boards in Flight Operations to the effect "lost sunglasses on aircraft 311" or "found headset on 5DG" because even pilots spread out their crap in the cockpit—then lose items. Don't spread out and at all costs, *resist the urge to stow items in the seatback pocket in front of you.*

At cruise during a recent flight from Cabo San Lucas, a flight attendant called the cockpit to let me know a passenger had found a passport in the seat pocket in front of him.

That meant that one of the passengers who'd just deplaned in Cabo was about to get an unpleasant surprise as he reached the front of the Mexican Customs Clearance line: *I left my passport on the plane.* Good luck clearing Customs there in Los Cabos and back in the United States (insider tip: I keep a copy of my birth certificate in my flight bag. That will get me back into the United States if my passport, which I keep on my person when I'm out of the US, is lost or stolen).

So just don't stow anything in the seatback pocket—or on the floor, because during climb, descent and turns, objects will slide forward, aft and sideways and—I've seen it happen—other passengers will deplane with your property.

That brings us to another important awareness: your seat area is not clean. Yes, it's "cleaned" periodically, but that's more like "wiped" at best. If you asked flight attendants to summarize in a word the cleanliness of the cabin, seats, tray tables and fixtures, they'd probably say "gross," and I'd agree. That's because the passengers sitting in your seat before your flight may not have had any reservation about putting their feet on the tray table you're about to eat off of and, though we have changing tables in the lavs, there has probably been a diaper change enacted on your seat or tray table.

Don't believe me? Search the web with the terms "passenger shaming" for photographs of exactly what I'm warning you about. You'll see why hand sanitizer and if you can find them, disinfectant wipes are a must-carry in flight.

Once you're seated and belted, your personal items stowed, it's time for the flight you've been prepping for. Remember, *you* are in control of your fate: you've made sensible preflight choices, you navigated the airport gauntlet successfully, you're settled in with your valuables and your inflight diversions (this book to share the hilarious[5] cartoons with your crew) such as reading material, music, digital diversions.

I appreciate—and you should too—that the aircraft environment is new to you and will naturally feel a little closed in, depending upon the size of the aircraft you're in.

That feeling is perfectly normal and everyone has that sensation at times in certain situations. That's the dentist office for me, because I'm only there twice a year and I'm not really sure of what's going to happen nor how it will feel. The point is, we all accommodate the worried feelings, not by denying them, but by thinking through them (I know I'm not going to be in the dentist's chair longer than an

---

[5] Okay, that's just me. But still.

hour) and persevere to a satisfactory outcome.

Once you're seated on board, you're prepped and ready to claim the payoff for your diligent forethought, in the form of a new means of travel at your fingertips. But even at that moment, you have choices: if you try flying and don't care for the experience, you never have to fly again if you don't want to, and with justification, but the decision will be based on known experience, not fear of the unknown.

I have faith that you'll tolerate the flight just fine and probably, you'll enjoy not only the flight, but future trips that were out of your reach before you became a capable flyer.

And that, my friend, is what I want you to be thinking as you're seated, waiting for flight. Let me handle the rest up front—that's what you've paid me and my crew to do, and we're good at what we do. Let's get underway.

Pushback and Taxi

Cabin: You may hear the entry door close. There may be some mechanical, whining sounds as auxiliary pumps are started for hydraulic power for brakes and steering. The lights may or may not flash briefly as power is shifted from an external source to on-board power.

Cockpit: We've been cleared to push back, so I've released the brakes and tell the ground crewman we're ready for him to begin pushing us back with the ground tug.

Cabin: You may feel a slight bump as the pushback begins, then the airflow will lessen a bit.

Cockpit: We've been cleared to start engines by the ground crew and when I relay that clearance to the First Officer (FO), he reconfigures the pneumatic flow away from the air conditioning systems and to the engine starters for engine start. I'll call for number two engine and he'll activate the starter.

Cabin: You may hear the engine spooling up to idle thrust, then maybe another electrical shift as an engine generator comes on line. More airflow resumes as one air conditioning system begins to receive air supply from the operating engine.

Cockpit: After pushback, I set the brakes and the ground crew clears the area. I call for number one engine start.

Cabin: The backwards motion eases to a stop. You may hear the other engine winding up to idle power, then full airflow will be restored.

Cockpit: I'll say, "bottoms," meaning I'm about to check the rudder pedals for unrestricted travel left and right so keep your feet clear." The FO will say "tops," meaning he'd about to pull the yoke back to test the elevator controls, then the control wheel left and right to ensure the ailerons are free and clear.

When I was an FO, with certain fat captains I'd pull back the yoke deliberately fast enough to smack their big gut. One large old guy asked me, "Whatcha tryin' to do, boy, loop it?"

The FO will ask me, "Flaps clear?" to be sure I'm ready to have the wing configured, and my standard answer is, "You bet."

Cabin: You may hear another mechanical sound of flap drives repositioning the flaps and leading edge slats on the wing to takeoff position. You may see the ailerons and wing spoilers raise as the FO checks full motion of these flight controls. We'll gradually ease into taxi speed, following the tower's taxi instructions to the takeoff runway.

Cockpit: Final pre-takeoff checks (see previous chapter) are accomplished, aircraft weight, speeds and departure procedure verified.

Cabin: Flight attendants will make their final pre-takeoff cabin walk-through to be sure all seatbelts are fastened and the cabin configured properly for takeoff, then they'll take their seats on the crew jumpseats.

Takeoff

Cabin: You'll hear the engines spool up to takeoff power. The jet will accelerate gradually on a longer runway, more rapidly on a shorter runway. Takeoff thrust takes into account many variables, but one goal is to limit engine wear by using only the thrust setting required rather than full power. So, acceleration and climb rates will vary as the takeoff power, flap settings and speeds are tailored to the optimum for that particular takeoff.

Cockpit: I'm checking for normal engine indications, normal acceleration and the takeoff clear-path ahead. At the designated speed, I'll "rotate," or in more mainstream terms, ease back on the control yoke carefully and hold the takeoff position until we're well clear of the runway. Then, I will increase pitch only as required to keep a constant speed to what we call "clean-up altitude," the height above the ground where I lower the nose so that we can accelerate to safe maneuvering speed with the flaps and slats retracted. As we accelerated through the speed gates, I call for flaps to be retracted and we climb at clean (no leading or trailing edge flaps) maneuvering speed.

Cabin: You may hear the "clunking" sound of gear retraction. Pitch will increase, then stabilize, then the nose will lower and you may sense acceleration again. You may hear the hydraulic motors driving flap and slat motors to retract those high lift devices into their stowed position. You may sense a slight rate of acceleration as we attain climb speed.

Your ears may sense the pressure change as the cabin slowly rises to the proper cruise pressurization: the aircraft cannot sustain sea level air pressure at altitude, so the automatic pressurization system gradually raises the cabin to a habitable pressure differential between inside and outside the pressure hull.

You may experience banking turns of up to thirty degrees, which is considered "standard rate" for maneuvering and which is expected by air traffic control to comply with the departure navigation restrictions.

Cockpit: We level off at cruise altitude and set the proper cruise thrust setting. All systems getting a once over: we used to call that a "HEFOE" (pronounced "he-foe") check in the Air Force: hydraulics, electrical system, fuel, oxygen, engines get a close look for proper indications. Navigation, weather scan, fuel burn and traffic watch are the main tasking for the cockpit crew.

Cabin: Your cabin crew will go about preparation for their inflight service. Insider Tip: if your personal electronic device needs charging, plug it in now. Once the maximum current draw is reached by the passenger power port system, no other devices will be able to draw electricity until someone unplugs. First come, first served with the power ports and the inflight WIFI: first one to use either gets the service.

Cockpit: I'll make a PA to the cabin describing our route of flight, arrival time and destination weather. This screed is so canned from having done it for over 26 years that I could do it in my sleep: the destination weather in my PA is always "partly cloudy" so if we arrive in rain, that's the part that's cloudy. If it's sunny, well, good. I also make up a temperature I think it should be but if it's not, well, by the time you discover it I'll already be a hundred miles away on my next flight leg anyway.

That's it, you made it to cruise! The rest is easy. Enjoy the view, keep your personal items securely in their place so nothing gets lost. I sure hope you have a window seat so you can watch the perfect tapestry below scrolling by below.

Inflight Mythology

I still remember my first flight as a nine-year-old, wide-eyed kid who loved all things about flying and aviation. I simply could not wait for that seatbelt sign to go off after takeoff because my big brother and I had a few items we planned to launch from the airplane toilet into thin air from way up in the sky. We just knew the lav would flush into the atmosphere and had big plans for that toilet.

What a total disappointment the reality was. But, I was just a kid. Here are a few adult myths that are just as baseless.

If the Engines Fail in Flight, the Aircraft will Plummet to the Earth: Actually, no; if both engines failed, we'd set up a gentle glide which would give us roughly three times our altitude in glide range: 30,000 feet of altitude would easily give us 90 miles of glide range. That's more than enough to either restart the engines or find a suitable runway to safely land on.

The Mile High Club: Puh-*leeze*, the lav is disgusting, not to mention tiny. Don't even think about it, and don't try, or a crewmember is likely to intervene. Seriously.

Airlines restrict cabin airflow to save money: This misguided notion may have originated in the 1960s when less advanced jet engines were more susceptible to airflow and fuel flow effects. Now, modern high-bypass engines have plenty of bleed air and state-of-the-art pressurization systems regulate temperature and pressure without manual restrictions.

Airflow is constant, drawn in through the engines, circulated through the cabin, then channeled through the forward equipment compartment to draw heat from electrical components to flow around the cargo compartment, warming it to a comfortable range for live animals, then overboard. No, airlines don't tamper with that vital airflow. In fact, that function is automated and works well.

Free Stuff from the Flight Attendants: Here's the thing. Despite what your friend of a friend's Uncle Fred said, flight attendants are serious about inflight disturbances which are often connected to excess alcohol consumption. So, don't expect free drinks.

But here's a secret: the basics of "please" and "thank you" will serve you well in flight when dealing with our hard-working cabin crews. That includes removing your headphones, listening to what they say, what they may ask you, and responding promptly and courteously.

Airlines will "hold" a connecting flight for you: Say I fly the noon departure to Seattle, and you're planning to connect onto that flight—but you're late inbound. You be the airline planner: would you "hold" my flight, knowing that 160 passengers in Seattle have connections in DFW and are counting on me to get them to DFW in time to connect? And that we have another flight to Seattle an hour after mine leaves? Would you "hold" a flight?

Aircraft doors can be opened in flight: Aircraft doors are designed as "plug" types. That means, pressure inside being greater than pressure outside (rewind to the pressurization differential discussion in this chapter) holds them closed in flight. So, no—just, no.

The Autopilot does most of the flying in flight: Certainly, the autopilot is preferable to many hours of pilot concentration to keep the wings level in flight, especially at higher altitudes where the margin between high and low speed stall is fairly narrow. But I've had flights to both coasts. where both autopilots failed and the FO and I took fifteen minutes shifts hand-flying to exacting altitude and airspeed standards. Wasn't fun, but it was safe and within regulations.

In the crucial approach regime, in the worst weather and winds, on my jet it's all hand-flown by the captain. I prefer it that way: I can fly just fine to a safe touchdown in all conditions my aircraft is rated to fly in, and I'd prefer to rely on my own flight experience than any automated system.

If you dress up to travel, you might be upgraded: The likelihood is nil for a couple reasons. First, airlines don't cater amenities and food for seats that are empty in First Class. Second, the airline manifest specifies who's to sit where, and flight attendants are not likely to increase the workload of the First Class cabin crew. Finally, the vast majority of vacant First Class seats are claimed by frequent flyers using their program points.

A "smooth" landing is a "good" landing; a "firm" landing is a "bad" landing: Touchdown feel has nothing to do with good and bad on landing. The requirement is to be on speed, on centerline, and on aim-point. Often, winds or runway conditions dictate a firm touchdown versus a "grease job:" a wet runway demands positive contact to avoid hydroplaning, and crosswinds can require a firm touchdown. Short runways require a touchdown early in the normal touchdown zone, firm or not.

Descent and Approach

Cockpit: About 200 miles from landing, we'll confirm our arrival routing and brief the expected instrument arrival and approach. We'll crosscheck and verify the arrival points, including altitude and speed restrictions. I'll take a minute to familiarize myself with the airport diagram to plan our taxi-in, even though I've been to most airports we serve dozens of times before. I visualize the sequencing of descent and approach and verify that my HUD is set up properly. I'll call back to the cabin and give them a heads-up that we'll be landing in twenty minutes or so, then turn on the seatbelt sign.

Cabin: You may sense a change in speed—usually a deceleration—which means we're transitioning to arrival sequencing from standard cruise speeds. Eventually, the nose will dip as we start descent. Shortly thereafter, the seatbelt sign will come on if it wasn't on already. This would be a good time to ensure all of your belongings are securely stowed in your hand-carried bag. The flight attendants will pass through the cabin collecting service items and refuse. They'll check to be sure all tray tables are stowed and all hand-carried luggage stowed for landing.

Cockpit: As we descend and decelerate, we'll reconfigure the plane for approach speed flight, using the leading edge and trailing edge flaps. We'll be sure we've tuned in the proper navigation aids on the ground and that our on-board navigation systems are set for the correct approach.

Cabin: As we descend into denser air at the lower altitudes, you might hear more wind noise from the slipstream. But that will subside as we slow the aircraft.

You may hear the hydraulic pumps powering the flap drives as we extend flaps and slats incrementally as we slow. You may see these devices extend from the leading and trailing edge of the wing.

You may hear a rumbling sound and notice large panels raise up from a flush position on the wings. Those are speed brakes and they help us slow down to approach speed or any lower speed assigned by air traffic control.

Landing and Taxi-in

Cockpit: Once we are cleared for the approach and cleared to land, we'll track the glideslope and azimuth to the runway using all available means: on-board navigation systems, ground-based navigation signals, and visual indicators. At a thousand feet above the ground, I will call stabilized if we meet the parameters: on speed, correct descent rate, on course, fully configured and checklists complete.

If we are not—and sometimes extraneous conditions may leave one or more parameter open—there's no problem: we simply discontinue the approach and request vectors around the traffic pattern for another approach. This is called a "Go-Around" and it is a perfectly nominal maneuver, even if we are close to the ground.

Sometimes, spacing between airplanes on final mandates a go-around. That is, perhaps the aircraft landing ahead of us slowed down too soon, compressing the interval between our aircraft and theirs, leaving insufficient spacing. We simply go around.

If that need arises, or if either pilot is dissatisfied with the approach for any reason, I will say (and either pilot can say), "Go-around." I'll add power, stop our descent, retract flaps to an intermediate setting and when clear of the ground and climbing, I'll call for gear retraction and we'll climb to the specified traffic pattern altitude.

Cabin (on a go-around): You'll feel the descent stop, perhaps abruptly, and the engines spool up to a higher power setting, as we accelerate and climb. You may hear the whine of flap motors as the flaps are repositioned, and the thud of landing gear retracting and gear doors closing.

Remember, a go-around is routine, just not very common because the air traffic control system works so efficiently most of the time. Relax—we'll simply fly around the traffic pattern and set up for another approach.'

Cockpit: at 500 feet above the ground on a continued approach, the pilot not flying the aircraft will evaluate the approach performance in terms of stability standards in roll, pitch, descent and azimuth. If all requirements are met, the pilot will state aloud, "stable, target, sinking 700."[6]

Cabin: The engine sound may vary as power adjustments are made to accommodate surface winds for landing. Small bank corrections may be made—you can see an aileron rise or dip and perhaps one of the wing panels might rise slightly, briefly—they are now acting as "spoilers," helping boost control response at lower airspeeds. Ground details and airport cues may be visible: approach lights, airport property.

Cockpit: Over the proper touchdown point, at about fifty feet above the runway, I'll "rotate" the aircraft (ease back slightly on the control yoke to raise the nose) and thereby "flare" the aircraft, meaning put it into the touchdown attitude. Simultaneously, I'll manually reduce thrust to idle to touch down with no power on the aircraft.

When we touch down on the two main gear located at the wing root, I'll watch for automatic spoiler deployment which the other pilot will confirm. This brings up all of the spoiler panels on top of the wings to eliminate any lift generated by the wings, thereby settling all of the aircraft

---

[6] "Stable" refers to the standards set by the airline, "target" refers to the required approach airspeed, and "sink" refers to the rate of descent, which also has limits.

weight on the main landing gear to speed braking action.

As I ease the control yoke toward neutral pitch, I'll deploy the thrust reversers on both engines, channeling engine thrust forward for braking purposes. I'll steer the jet with my feet on the rudder pedals, maintaining centerline with the rudder and the nosewheel until we are slowed to taxi speed. I'll begin manual braking by pressing on the rudder pedals to slow us further.

Modern runways have "high speed turnoffs" angled such that we can make the turn off of the runway at up to ninety knots, but I wait till we're between sixty and seventy to be conservative. At eighty knots, I'll reduce the reverse thrust to be in forward idle by sixty knots.

Once we're clear of the runway, I'll call for the after-landing checklist and the FO will begin reconfiguring the aircraft for taxi-in and parking. We both listen careful for taxi instructions and verify all taxi clearances.

Cabin: Just prior to touchdown, you'll likely hear the engines become quiet at flight idle, their lowest thrust output. You may sense the slight nose pitch up of the "flare" maneuver right before touch down. We'll touch down, the spoilers will pop up on the wings and in a moment you will hear the engines spool up again to reverse thrust power. You'll feel the brakes when we apply them, then you'll feel us turn off the runway and begin taxiing. You'll hear the whine of hydraulic motors as we retract the flaps and slats.

As we taxi in, the cabin crew will make a PA welcoming you to our arrival city and letting you know when it is permissible to use electronic devices. When given the all-clear to use your phone, be sure it's on and switched out of the airplane mode. Check your airline app to confirm your arrival gate and baggage claim.

Flight attendants may specify a baggage claim area if they have that information, but they might not have it available. Your airline's app will provide you with the most current gate and baggage claim information, as well as connecting gate information if you are making a connection. If you are connecting on to another flight but don't have the airline app, Google your next flight number to verify the departure gate.

As you taxi in, confirm that all of your belongings are stowed and that you've left no personal property on the floor, in the seat or the seatback pocket.

After we park, the seatbelt sign will be turned off, but just stay comfortably seated because it will take a few minutes for the jetbridge to mate up to the aircraft and for the entry door to be opened.

After that, all of the passengers seated forward of your row will need to deplane and that will take at least another ten minutes. Relax, check around your seat to be sure you haven't left anything behind and wait your turn.

When I deadhead, I typically wait until everyone has deplaned before I gather my things and leave, more as a courtesy to others: I don't have the stress of connections or people waiting for me.

When I'm in the cockpit, I wait until everyone has deplaned and the flight attendants file off, out of respect to them: the captain should be last to leave. It's a privilege to be the captain and an honor to be the last on board.

Quick Reference Summary

- There are standard sounds and feeling associated with the routine progress of a flight. Review the sensations of flight listed in this section.
- Most of the mythology related to air travel is false (review that section here).
- Don NOT spread your personal belongings out around your seat. Rather, stow any item after you are done using it.
- Stow NOTHING EVER in the seatback pocket.
- If your electronic devices need charging, plug them in immediately when cleared to do so because once the cabin maximum amperage is reached, you will not get electrical power from your outlet. Ditto the WIFI: first come, first served. Log on as soon as permitted if you need to upload or download.
- A go-around is a normal, non-emergency maneuver. Review what will happen and be prepared.
- A "soft" landing is not necessarily a good landing.

A hard landing is not a bad landing. Prepare for both.

- After landing when permitted, switch your phone from "airplane mode" and check for your arrival gate and baggage claim via the airline app or Google.

- After the aircraft is parked and the seatbelt sign is turned off, just remain comfortably seated. Don't be "that guy" who jumps up, clogs the aisle but goes nowhere..

10 GOING FORWARD

At first glance, that title seems like a paradox for a last chapter, but "Going Forward" is a key concept in your flight journey: there's no quick fix, instant magic that dispels fear of flying—nor should there be, because the fear has deep, justifiable roots.

But just like flight itself, the evolution from wishing to fly and safely, comfortably doing so is a long-term, accretive process of building blocks, new insights, manageable, small steps and incremental progress. There will be setbacks, but there will be advances. There will be anxious moments, but there will be progress to celebrate.

Working through your very rational concerns is like learning to play a musical instrument or speaking another language: there are no shortcuts—you either practice playing the tuba, or you never learn. You read and drill in French, or you'll never speak the language.

I know, it's a stretch—I just really like this cartoon.

That's the nature of flight: I didn't learn to fly quickly or easily. It was a fight most of the way, a struggle that yielded only to practice, repetition, good guidance, more repetition, more practice, and constant, recursive concentration and determination. And it never ends.

The same is demanded of you: reread this book[7], imprint the facts and information in this book in your awareness. The fear won't vanish, but you will own a powerful countermeasure—knowledge—to manage the anxiety. When, in your own good time, you're prepared to fly, you'll do so on a more level playing field, having ownership of the facts about your flight, your aircraft, your crew, your airline, the air traffic control system, the sensations and sounds of flight, how to prepare, when to get to the airport, where to secure the latest flight and travel information, how to negotiate security screening, boarding,

---

[7] The compact size of this book was a deliberate design choice—it'll fit in any bag for reading anywhere—especially in flight if you need reassurance.

even your seating area and finally, even deplaning (don't be "that guy").

Make aviation an area you're familiar with, that you are knowledgeable about. Track your scheduled flight ahead of time for five days, maybe a week: that's your first step toward privileging the known (the flight operates safely, routinely, without a hitch) over the unknown ("what if").

Visit an aviation museum, see the hardware up close, the airfoils, engines. Read an airline trade periodical publication (*Aviation Week & Space Technology* is the gold standard) and see what amazing safety improvements are being made all the time to advance the already spectacular safety record of air travel.

Tour an airport, watch passenger traffic and flight operations. Many airports have tours, some have observation areas near flight operations (e.g., DFW Airport has a park called "Founder's Plaza" near the approach end of the west runways, with speakers sharing the tower-to-cockpit transmissions of landing aircraft you can watch) and take the mystery of flight away from the runaway imagination that fills in the blanks with unfounded dread at 3am.

There are social media communities of like-minded folks who struggle with fear of flying. They support each other, share assets, ideas, results, and just the commonality of knowing you're not alone in your concern. Lurk or participate but mostly, learn and replace toxic thought patterns with constructive information.

I have written extensively about airline flight from a pilot's perspective to help fill in the blanks for you as a passenger, and the majority of those articles and topics are discussed more extensively on my blog

www.JetHead.Wordpress.com

which is a not-for-profit (you may see an ad for one of my

airline crew cartoon books, but that's the extent of my commercialism) site explaining airline flight.

There's a contact form on the "About" page of the blog where you can send me any suggestions, even topics that I might cover in future editions of this book. I hope you'll share your ideas to make this book more useful and helpful. What would *you* like to see covered in future editions?

Finally, when you find yourself confidently strolling through the airport between flights, be proud of what you've accomplished and enjoy the new world of travel you've entered and opened for yourself and your family. Know that I'm rooting for you and that I appreciate your monumental achievement.

You won't likely see me in the terminal—I've made a science out of being invisible, remember?—but if you're on board one of my flights, do stop by the cockpit and say hi. I'd love to share in your success.

Until then, safe travels.

GET THE WHOLE
AIRLINE CARTOON COLLECTION

$7.99
Order Here:

9-16-17

ABOUT THE AUTHOR

Chris Manno earned his USAF wings after college and spent seven years as a pilot and officer based in Okinawa then Honolulu, flying throughout the Pacific, Asia and the United States.

At the world's largest airline he has flown and holds airline pilot ratings in the DC-9, DC-10, MD-80, F-100 and B-737, with over 20,000 flight hours.

He earned a doctorate in English from Texas Christian University and teaches writing at Texas Wesleyan University in addition to flying a full schedule as B-737 captain.

Get another copy of this book here:

Or Search Amazon.com

Made in the USA
Lexington, KY
14 October 2017